What people are saying about …

"Are you spiritually empty and searching for something more? Perhaps you're missing out on God's presence and power through the Holy Spirit. In *Forgotten God*, Francis Chan imparts a life-changing message on the power of the Holy Spirit and His desire to unleash Himself into our daily lives."

**Craig Groeschel,** founding pastor of LifeChurch.tv and author
of *It: How Churches and Leaders Can Get It and Keep It*

"It has often been said that the Holy Spirit is the Cinderella of the God-head. But no church and no Christian can be healthy or attain maturity without a life lived in and led by the Spirit. Francis Chan's latest book is a timely reminder and engaging encouragement to get intimately acquainted with the Forgotten God."

**Simon Ponsonby,** Bible teacher, pastor, and author of
*And the Lamb Wins, More,* and *God Inside Out*

Praise for …

## Francis Chan

"Chan writes with infectious exuberance, challenging Christians to take the Bible seriously."

**Publishers Weekly**

"Francis Chan leaves you wanting more … more of the matchless Jesus who offers radical life for all right now."

**Louie Giglio,** visionary architect, director of Passion Conferences, and author of *I Am Not, but I Know I AM*

"Francis's life reflects authentic leadership tempered by a deep compassion for the lost, the last, the littlest, and the least. It's all because this man, my friend, is an ardent and devoted disciple of his Savior. Francis guides us down the path toward an uncommon intimacy with Jesus—an intimacy which can't help but change the world around us!"

**Joni Eareckson Tada,** best-selling author and speaker

"Whether in the pulpit or on the page, Francis Chan effuses love for Jesus Christ and demonstrates practical ways to throw off lukewarm Christianity and embrace full-on, passionate love for God."

**Kirk Cameron,** actor and author of *Still Growing*

# REMEMBERING THE FORGOTTEN GOD

## An Interactive Workbook for Individual or Small Group Study

### FRANCIS CHAN
and Mark Beuving

David C Cook®

*transforming lives together*

REMEMBERING THE FORGOTTEN GOD
Published by David C Cook
4050 Lee Vance Drive
Colorado Springs, CO 80918 U.S.A.

David C Cook U.K., Kingsway Communications
Eastbourne, East Sussex BN23 6NT, England

Scripture taken from *The Holy Bible, English Standard Version.* Copyright © 2000; 2001 by Crossway
Bibles, a division of Good News Publishers. Used by permission. All rights reserved. Scripture
quotations marked KJV are taken from the King James Version of the Bible. (Public Domain.)

LCCN 2009943453
ISBN 978-1-4347-0088-9
eISBN 978-1-4347-0209-8

The Team: Don Pape, Karen Lee-Thorp, Amy Kiechlin, Sarah Schultz, Caitlyn York, Karen Athen
Cover Design: Jim Elliston

Printed in the United States of America

First Edition 2010

13 14 15 16 17 18 19 20 21 22

012717

# CONTENTS

# GETTING STARTED

To a frightening extent, the church has forgotten about the Holy Spirit. We talk about Him from time to time, and we believe that He is actually living inside of us, but what difference do you see between a typical Christian, who has the Holy Spirit, and a typical non-Christian, who doesn't?

Due in large part to our Western mind-set, we tend to assume that God won't work supernaturally in our lives. Sure, the Spirit did some crazy things in the book of Acts, but He doesn't work that way anymore. Or does He? One thing is certain: We will never know the power of the Spirit until we open our lives to follow His leading.

Without the supernatural power of God in our lives, we remain incredibly ordinary. Our churches remain ordinary. At times we will attempt big things for God, but we don't expect anything supernatural. Our natural tendency is to work in our own strength rather than relying on the Holy Spirit, and the results are not surprising.

How do we explain the absence of the Spirit's power in the church today? Is the Holy Spirit weaker now than He was in New Testament times? Or have we simply restructured our lives to be safer, more comfortable, and more self-dependent?

This workbook is about exploring the person of the Holy Spirit and reflecting on His power to work in and through *you*. It's not enough to believe in the Spirit's power generally or His plan for the church as a whole. It's time for each of us to develop a relationship with the Spirit of the living God and begin to follow His leading in our daily lives.

As you work through these seven sessions, you will study the person and work of the

Holy Spirit. But rather than focusing on doctrine in an abstract sense, you will be asked to consider the implications for your life, question your motives, challenge your assumptions, and ultimately learn to love, follow, and rely on the Spirit of God.

Before you start, ask yourself if you really want to be changed. Studying the most powerful being imaginable is bound to make you uneasy about certain aspects of your life. Do you really want to meet Him in the days and weeks ahead?

It is impossible to encounter the Holy Spirit of God and not be changed.

## How to Get the Most Out of This Workbook

There are a few different ways to use this workbook. You can work through the study as an individual, as a part of a small group, or even during a weekend retreat. I've made some suggestions for using the workbook in each of these settings below.

This workbook is designed to work hand in hand with the *Forgotten God* book and the *Forgotten God DVD Study Resource*. Ideally, you will read the relevant chapter from *Forgotten God,* then go through the corresponding session in this workbook, watching the appropriate video from the DVD when prompted. Use the Reflection pages at the end of each session to elaborate on any additional thoughts your study prompted.

But while that is the most thorough way of studying the material, the workbook also stands on its own. You'll notice that each session refers to the book and the DVD, but you can get a lot out of this workbook without those resources.

### *Using the Workbook on Your Own*

The most effective way to use this workbook is to go through it on your own, even if you're also going to discuss it in a group or on a retreat. Many of the questions are personal, and taking the time to read through the sessions and think through how each question should affect your life will give the study depth and immediate personal application.

If you have the *Forgotten God* book, I suggest reading the corresponding chapter before starting each session of this workbook. If you have the *Forgotten God DVD Study Resource*, you'll notice that each session prompts you to watch the appropriate video at a particular point in the study. I recommend watching the video when prompted, then working through the rest of the session.

## *Using the Workbook in a Small Group*

If you're working through the material as a part of a small group, the best way to begin is by working through each chapter on your own before the group discussion (see the section for individuals above). Reading and thinking through each session on your own before your group meets will better prepare you for the discussion. I recommend writing in your answers and any notes or questions you may have before you meet with your group, and then adding to your notes based on the discussion.

When you meet with your group, establish a discussion leader. (If you've been chosen for this task, see the "Notes for Discussion Leaders" at the end of this workbook.) This person doesn't need to have all the answers. (Who does when it comes to studying the Holy Spirit?) The discussion leader will simply guide the conversation and decide when to move on to the next question.

For each session, discuss the numbered questions as a group. Feel free to read a section out loud if the questions are unclear. Some of the questions can be answered quickly, but I encourage you to take your time, giving multiple group members a chance to share. This will enrich the discussion, and different perspectives will often give you more ideas for practical application.

At a specific point in each session, you will be prompted to play the *Forgotten God DVD Study Resource*. I suggest getting one copy for your group and watching the videos together while you meet. If you do it this way, individual group members will work through the material on their own and wait to watch the videos until the group meets. When you get together, discuss the numbered questions until you are prompted to watch the DVD. After the video, discuss the rest of the questions.

It may be helpful to arrange chairs in a U shape around the television so that everyone can see the screen when you watch the video, and so that everyone can see one another as you discuss your thoughts before and after the video. If this arrangement is possible, then you won't need to move chairs during your meeting.

Most importantly, I encourage you to be honest with the members of your group. If your desire is to grow and change, you will need the other group members to pray for you, support you, and at times challenge your thinking. By opening up to one another, your whole group will become more open to the Spirit's leading.

## Using the Workbook for a Weekend Retreat

Some churches will want to use this workbook as a part of a weekend retreat. If that's the case, the retreat leaders have some decisions to make: Do you want to use the *Forgotten God DVD Study Resource* for all or part of the main sessions? Maybe you'll want to plan messages around the material covered in each session (if that's the case, I highly recommend reading the *Forgotten God* book). You may just want to plan out seven meeting times during the course of the weekend, play the DVD for the whole group, and then have everyone break off into smaller groups to discuss the material.

However you choose to do it, I recommend dividing the large group into smaller groups and setting aside seven different small-group meeting times. Small groups of four to six people give everyone a chance to talk. People who are shy about talking in large groups are often more comfortable talking in small ones. And people who tend to dominate discussions in large groups more easily find balance with others in small circles.

You'll probably want to address the entire group at least a few times during the weekend to give them some thoughts, but giving them time to meet in smaller groups will be important. Group members will want to read the section for small groups above, and discussion leaders will want to read the "Notes for Discussion Leaders" section at the end of this workbook.

Discussion leaders don't need to be experts either in the content or in leading groups, because they will fairly quickly learn how to guide a conversation with only four to six other people. Ideally, you will choose discussion leaders ahead of time, but if you can't, it's surprising how often these groups can choose the most natural leader among them after getting to know each other for only a brief time. You can read aloud the job description of a discussion leader (see the end of this workbook) and pray for the Holy Spirit to guide the groups in choosing discussion leaders. Groups will often unanimously choose someone among them to do the job once they know what it involves.

It's a good idea for people to stick with the same group for the whole series so that they get to know each other.

Because small groups may be scattered around your meeting area with chairs in small circles, you'll need to decide when and how to watch the video together. It takes time and organization if people have to stop their discussion, move from one location to another, watch the video, and then move back to their discussion circle. Because the video is brief, you may find that the easiest plan for a large group is to view the video all together at the beginning of each meeting period and then scatter the small groups for discussion for the rest of the period.

# SESSION I

# I'VE GOT JESUS. WHY DO I NEED THE SPIRIT?

For more information on the material in this session, read the Introduction and chapter 1 of the book *Forgotten God: Reversing Our Tragic Neglect of the Holy Spirit*.

Have you ever felt like you're missing something? Like you're getting by, but your life lacks something crucial, something extraordinary?

Somehow, we in the American church have managed to systematically neglect the power of the Holy Spirit. And the sad thing is that many people haven't even noticed. An increasing number of us recognize that there's a problem, but most of us still have no idea what we're missing out on.

In general, we don't value the Holy Spirit. But Jesus did: "It is the Spirit who gives life; the flesh is no help at all" (John 6:63). And from a biblical standpoint, you simply cannot live the Christian life without the Spirit of God. Paul says, "Anyone who does not have the Spirit of Christ does not belong to him" (Rom. 8:9). We have no idea the power available to us through the Spirit. Romans 8:11 tells us, "If the Spirit of him who raised Jesus from the dead dwells in you, he who raised Christ Jesus from the dead will also give life to your mortal bodies through his Spirit who dwells in you." Think of the power that it took to raise Jesus from the dead. Paul says that the same Holy Spirit who brings life out of death *lives inside of us!*

How have we missed this? I'm guessing that you've heard these verses before. But most of us have probably come to accept our experience of the Christian life as normal. It's time to question what we've always thought. None of us is as biblical in our thinking as we'd like to believe.

Think about it for a minute. Why do you believe what you believe? What process do you follow in forming your beliefs? Most of us would probably say that our beliefs are based on the Word of God, but really, our beliefs are often born more out of convenience and consistency than a careful study of the Scriptures. This is certainly true when it comes to our views about the Holy Spirit.

Chances are, you owe most of what you believe about the Holy Spirit to what you've seen and heard from the people around you. It's important to learn from other people, but at times we need to challenge our way of thinking. We are all in constant need of bringing our lives in line with the Scriptures.

1. Take a minute and list some of your beliefs about the Holy Spirit. (Even if you don't consider yourself a theologian, most of us have at least a few ideas about who the Holy Spirit is and what He does.)

2. Being as open as possible, do you think your beliefs are shaped more by the Scriptures or by what you've come to experience as the normal Christian life? What makes you say that?

At some point, we all need to get past what we think we know about the Spirit. If we are going to rediscover the power and presence of the Holy Spirit, we will need to begin listening to His voice and following His leading—not in the ways we think He should speak and lead, but in whatever He may call us to do.

 **If you have the *Forgotten God DVD Study Resource,* watch the video for session 1 now, particularly if you are meeting with a group. After the video, work through the rest of this section.**

In the busyness of our lives, we have developed a remarkable ability to miss the obvious. We overanalyze the things that don't deserve a second thought, and we blow right past the clear, obvious, important things in life.

We assume that we know what the Christian life ought to look like. But have you ever sat down and considered the way Scripture describes the Spirit-filled life?

3. The following passages offer a brief overview of what the Holy Spirit does in a person's life. Quickly flip through these passages and make some notes. (If you don't want to look up all of these passages, feel free to choose just a few at random.)

Acts 1:4–8　*you shall be baptized with the Holy Spirit*

Acts 2:1–13　*filled with the Holy Spirit and began to speak with other tongues as the spirit gave them utterance*

Acts 4:31  And when they had prayed, the place where they were assembled together was shaken; and they were all filled with the Holy Spirit, and they spoke the word of God with boldness.

Romans 8:1–17  Walk according to the Spirit
                    Spirit is life.

Romans 8:26–27  Spirit Himself makes intercession for us with groanings which cannot be uttered.

Romans 15:13  Now may the God of hope fill you with all joy and peace in believing, that you may abound in hope by the power of the Holy Spirit.

1 Corinthians 2:12–14  The Spirit who is from God, that we might know the things that have been freely given to us by God. Holy Spirit teaches, comparing spiritual things with spiritual.
                    Spiritually discerned.

1 Corinthians 3:16  Do you not know that you are the temple of God and that the Spirit of God dwells in you.

1 Corinthians 6:9–11  washed and sanctified, justified in the name of the Lord Jesus and by the spirit of our God.

1 Corinthians 12:7–11

2 Corinthians 3:17–18

Galatians 4:4–7

Galatians 5:16–25

Ephesians 3:14–16

1 John 4:13

4. If you disregarded your own experiences and just read these passages, what would you expect to observe as the Holy Spirit entered a person's life?

5. For so many people in the church today, everyday life does not match these biblical descriptions. Why do you think that is?

The statement is so familiar to us that we sometimes overlook its significance: "The Spirit of God dwells in you" (Rom. 8:9). One obvious truth that we frequently overlook is that there should be a huge difference between someone who has the Spirit of God living inside of them and someone who does not.

Have you ever observed Christians and non-Christians interacting? In many cases, it is all but impossible to discern who has the Spirit and who doesn't. Sure, the Christians may be a little nicer or more morally conscientious, but is that really *all* the Holy Spirit came to do in our lives? Shouldn't the difference be supernatural?

Read Galatians 5:16–25.

Paul is telling the Galatians what the Christian life ought to look like. In Christ, we have been set free from the law. But without the law, how do we please God? How do we love our neighbors as ourselves? For Paul, the answer is simple: Walk by the Spirit.

6. According to Galatians 5:16–25, what does it look like to walk by the Spirit?

7. Based on what Paul says here, what should distinguish a Spirit-filled person from a non-Christian?

If the Holy Spirit is being neglected in our churches and in our lives, is it any wonder that we don't look much different from the rest of the world? Too often we work in our own strength to be the kind of people who stand out—the kind of people who look like Jesus. This is the right goal, but when we try to do this without relying on the Spirit, we're missing the whole point. Doesn't it strike you as odd that although we want to live out the attributes of Galatians 5:22–23, we don't rely on the Holy Spirit to produce the fruit *of the Spirit?*

Look at Galatians 5:16 again: "But I say, walk by the Spirit, and you will not gratify the desires of the flesh." Perhaps we've gotten so caught up in trying to live the Christian life that we've overlooked the Source. Life-change comes through the power of the Holy Spirit. At times we try so hard—but if we have forgotten about the Holy Spirit, then we're missing the whole point.

8. Every day, people try to live the "Spirit-filled" life without the Spirit. Based on your experience, what good things can we accomplish merely through human strength?

9. If the Spirit works through us, how should the supernatural results differ from
   what we can accomplish on our own?

I know that there are people in the church who live every day in the power of the Spirit, depending on and following Him in every aspect of life. Maybe you're one of those blessed few. Praise God if that's the case! But we all have room to grow. None of us has too much of the Spirit. We are all in danger of pursuing supernatural results through our own strength.

It's time for us to stop assuming that we know everything we need to know about the Holy Spirit. Some of us need to study a little deeper and find out who the Spirit is and what He does. This is an important step in the process. But all of us need to begin applying the obvious biblical truths about the Holy Spirit to our lives. Maybe you haven't missed the obvious doctrinally—maybe you've missed it practically. Until we actually apply a truth to our lives, we can't claim to believe it—at least not with any integrity.

Look again at the fruit of the Spirit listed in Galatians 5:22–23. Add to that list a host of other godly characteristics that we are called to pursue (such as faith, hope, compassion). These are not just abstract concepts. These fruits should be evident in our actions toward the people around us.

10. Don't just think about what the Holy Spirit can do for you. What are some
    clear and practical ways that the Spirit can work through you to bless the
    people around you?

Chapter 1 of the book *Forgotten God* ends with a powerful analogy about the confusion a caterpillar must experience:

> For all its caterpillar life, it crawls around a small patch of dirt and up and down a few plants. Then one day it takes a nap. A long nap. And then, what in the world must go through its head when it wakes up to discover it can *fly?* What happened to its dirty, plump little worm body? What does it think when it sees its tiny new body and gorgeous wings?
>
> As believers, we ought to experience this same kind of astonishment when the Holy Spirit enters our bodies. We should be stunned in disbelief over becoming a "new creation" with the Spirit living in us. As the caterpillar finds its new ability to fly, we should be thrilled over our Spirit-empowered ability to live differently and faithfully. (*Forgotten God*, 37)

11. For all practical purposes, we seem to have forgotten that the Holy Spirit is powerful—He radically transforms lives. Are you open to being transformed, no matter what that may mean for your life? If you do want to be changed, why do you desire this? If you don't, what is keeping you from desiring change?

12. Spend some time praying that God will give you the humility to be open to what He wants to teach you—even if it means you've spent years overlooking the obvious. Then ask Him to begin using these truths to change the way you live.

# REFLECTIONS ON ...

## I've Got Jesus. Why Do I Need the Spirit?

# SESSION 2

# WHAT ARE YOU AFRAID OF?

For more information on the material in this session,
read chapter 2 of the book *Forgotten God.*

Fear is an excellent motivator. Every American is taught from an early age to denounce fear. Our heroes are tough and fearless. We actually believe that the only thing we have to fear is fear itself. But let's face it: We're all far more affected by fear than we'd like to let on.

1. Think about a time in your life when you were afraid (whether the fear was irrational or legitimate). How did you feel? How did you respond?

If I asked you whether your theology was formed by truth or fear, I doubt anyone would answer "fear." But the Holy Spirit has become a controversial topic of discussion. Whole camps have formed around particular understandings of the Spirit. Most evangelical churches could be categorized as either charismatic or non-charismatic. And deviating from your camp's position could cause you to be questioned or even rejected. Changing your views about the Spirit could mean finding another church or group of friends.

2. Why do you think it is so easy to become defensive and fearful of change when it comes to the doctrine of the Holy Spirit?

It's natural to develop specific views about the Holy Spirit. But unfortunately, we typically develop stereotypes about the other camp. While some aspects of these stereotypes are based on fact, most of the time they're exaggerated at best and unfounded at worst.

When all we know about the other position is based on stereotypes, it breeds fear. It is this kind of fear that keeps us stationary. We're afraid to move from our position because we don't want to become "like them."

3. Try to figure out where you're at with this. Which camp (if any) do you most identify with regarding your established views of the Holy Spirit, and what fears and stereotypes do you have of the other camp?

4. Being as honest as possible, do you think those fears would keep you from changing your views and practices, even if you found that the Scriptures teach that your views are misguided? Why, or why not?

If you're not afraid of becoming like the other camp, there are other kinds of fears that keep us from what God has for us.

Most of us have experienced a time when we asked God to do something, but He did not come through in the way we expected. Maybe you're afraid that if you ask God for the Holy Spirit, nothing will happen. I'm sure that more of us are guilty of this than are willing to admit it. You read the Bible and don't see any reason why God couldn't do today what He did then. But you don't see the miraculous in your everyday life, so you're afraid that if you ask God for His Spirit, you'll be disappointed.

5. If you are motivated by a fear that God won't act when you ask Him to, what does that say about your view of God?

If you are afraid that the Holy Spirit won't show up when you ask Him to, start by assessing your requests in light of James 4:2–3: "You do not have, because you do not ask. You ask and do not receive, because you ask wrongly, to spend it on your passions." Sometimes God doesn't show up because we don't ask Him to. Sometimes God doesn't answer our requests because our motives are all wrong. Rather than praying for the things that God has promised to give us (like the Holy Spirit—see Luke 11:13) we pray that God will give us what we want.

Many of us need to earnestly check our hearts at this point. If you find yourself doubting that God can and will do the impossible, you need to reexamine your view of God. Try reading through the book of Acts. As you read, ask yourself whether or not you believe that the God you worship is the same God who worked in all of these incredible ways.

There is one other fear that we ought to address. Perhaps the only thing scarier than the Spirit not showing up is the thought that He will! What if the Holy Spirit started to act powerfully in your life? I'm concerned that most of us are not prepared for what that might mean.

**If you have the *Forgotten God DVD Study Resource,* watch the video for session 2, particularly if you are meeting with a group. After the video, work through the rest of this section.**

Ignorance can be bliss. If we don't know exactly what God wants us to do, we can maintain our current lifestyle and still manage a perception of godliness.

6. Imagine that the Holy Spirit took complete control of your life and showed you exactly what He wanted you to do. Why might the thought of actually following the Holy Spirit be scary?

Have you ever found yourself fearful of this? If so, describe what you thought and did.

Read Luke 18:18–30. The ruler in this story had been going about his life in peace. Apparently, he was really striving to keep God's commandments. He seems to have been sincere in asking Jesus about the path to eternal life. He was confident in his efforts. But (as we often find) Jesus' answer required more than he was prepared to give.

7. Why do you think the ruler was so surprised when Jesus told him to sell his possessions and give to the poor? What do you think he was expecting Jesus to say?

8. What did Jesus mean when He said "follow me" (v. 22)?

Do you think the ruler understood what Jesus meant by this? Why, or why not?

Just like the blackjack game mentioned in the video, Jesus acknowledges that it's more difficult to follow when a lot is at stake: "How difficult it is for those who have wealth to enter the kingdom of God!" (Luke 18:24). It's easier to go "all in" when we don't have much. In America, not many of us fall into that category.

9. Try to put yourself in the ruler's position. He was a wealthy man, yet he came to Jesus to learn what he should do. Picture yourself coming to Jesus and asking His Spirit to lead you in the right direction. Do you have any thoughts about what He might ask you to do?

10. Would you be willing to follow, no matter what that might mean? Why do you say that?

Most people are control freaks. It can be difficult to let someone else call the shots, especially when it comes to the way you live your life. "The truth is that the Spirit of the living God is guaranteed to ask you to go somewhere or do something you wouldn't normally want or choose to do" (*Forgotten God*, 50). Does that statement surprise you? No matter what plans we may have for our lives, none of us is perfectly in tune with God's will:

> For my thoughts are not your thoughts,
>> neither are your ways my ways, declares the LORD.
>
> For as the heavens are higher than the earth,
>> so are my ways higher than your ways
>> and my thoughts than your thoughts. (Isa. 55:8–9).

At this point, question yourself: Do you really believe that where the Holy Spirit would lead you is better than where you would lead yourself? That's a difficult question to answer, a question that the rest of this study will help you to answer. In fact, we will spend the rest of our lives becoming more and more convinced that God's way is the best way. For now, it's all about laying aside our fears and trusting the Spirit to lead us.

Fear paralyzes us for a variety of reasons. But there is one thing in particular that we actually should be afraid of when it comes to the Holy Spirit: "Do not quench the Spirit. Do not despise prophecies, but test everything; hold fast what is good" (1 Thess. 5:19–21). We shouldn't fear other people, the possibility that God won't show up, or the possibility that He will show up. But we should be afraid of quenching the Spirit. What hope does the church have if we actively suppress the power of God?

11. Read Ephesians 4:30. Write down a few aspects of your life that you think
    may grieve the Holy Spirit and hinder His work in and through you. Once
    you've written them down, stop and pray. Repent of those things and ask the
    Spirit to give you the strength to put those things to death.

In Luke 11, Jesus teaches His disciples how to pray. He tells them to ask, and it will be given to them; to seek, and they will find; to knock, and the door will be opened (v. 9). He says that every human father knows how to give good gifts to his children. And then He draws a powerful conclusion: "If you then, who are evil, know how to give good gifts to your children, how much more will the heavenly Father give the Holy Spirit to those who ask him!" (v. 13).

12. Spend some time in prayer. Ask God to remove your fears about following
    the Holy Spirit. Ask God to give you the Holy Spirit. Pray that the Spirit
    would show you what He wants you to do and pray that God would give
    you the strength and the heart to follow wherever He might lead.

# REFLECTIONS ON ...

## What Are You Afraid Of?

**SESSION 3**

# THEOLOGY OF THE HOLY SPIRIT 101

For more information on the material in this session,
read chapter 3 of the book *Forgotten God.*

Theology always pushes us in a particular direction. The knowledge of God is not neutral—it demands something of us. Every thought and belief in our minds leads us to some sort of action.

Unfortunately, we don't always grasp the significance of what we claim to believe. If we stop short of applying a truth to our lives, then we do not actually grasp that truth. Until our lives (and not just our beliefs) are changed, we are not doing theology.

Chapter 3 of *Forgotten God* says it like this:

> What you do and how you live are absolutely vital. Without action and fruit, all the theology in the world has little meaning. But theology is still important—what you believe absolutely determines how you act. So while good theology at its best can lead us to live godly lives, bad theology will

always point us in the wrong direction. When we study the
Holy Spirit, bad theology can lead to ineffective lives or,
worse yet, lives spent striving after what the Spirit of God
opposes. (64)

More important than what we know is how we act. Being a Christian isn't about knowing
a set of propositions—it's about knowing Christ and acting on His behalf in the world. But
our beliefs shape our actions. As we study the Holy Spirit, it's vitally important that our
understanding of who He is and what He does is accurate. If our understanding is misguided,
we could spend our whole lives on pursuits that grieve the Spirit. But once our theology is in
the right place (or at least headed in the right direction), we need to act on it.

1. Write down a few of the things that you've learned about the Holy Spirit in
   the last two sessions.

2. How should those truths start shaping the way you act?

Have you seen this happen yet? Place a check mark beside any of the actions you just listed that you've begun to see in your life.

 If you have the *Forgotten God DVD Study Resource,* watch the video for session 3, particularly if you are meeting with a group. After the video, come back and work through the rest of this section.

Think about the football-huddle analogy for a minute. Too often the church is like a football team that huddles, calls a play, and then sits on the bench—never to run the play that they got so excited about. Perhaps we've forgotten the Holy Spirit because we don't need Him. We don't need the Spirit for the huddle; we need Him when we step out of the huddle and run the play.

3. Think about your gathering of believers in light of the huddle analogy. Have you been running from the huddle to the bench? If so, in what ways?

4. God gave us the Spirit so that we might change the world through His power. How do you think the church would look if we all began "running the plays"?

5. How do you think the world would respond?

We're all capable of studying biblical truth in a way that makes us "smarter" but doesn't affect anything in our lives. On the other hand, we also have the ability to study in such a way that our lives are never the same because of what we've learned. The end result of this study could be that you walk away knowing more about the Holy Spirit. Or it could be that you walk away *knowing the Holy Spirit,* showing the people around you a Spirit-filled life. Only a life lived in the power of the Spirit can offer the world something better than what they have.

## Who the Spirit Is

The rest of this session is going to look a little different. Rather than focusing on a single passage, we're going to study some of the attributes of the Holy Spirit. The goal is to get you better acquainted with the Spirit. If you've never heard these truths before, then consider looking up the accompanying Scripture references. Allow these truths to form your understanding of the Spirit.

For many of us who grew up in the church, these attributes of the Spirit are very familiar—maybe you've even lost your sense of wonder. If that's you, I challenge you to approach these truths as if you've never heard them before. Ponder the Spirit until you find yourself in awe of Him. The most amazing part of this whole thing is that the very Spirit you are studying is actually *living inside of you!*

6. Read the following statements about the Holy Spirit. Take your time. Think about the practical implications of that particular attribute of the Spirit. If you want to spend more time on each point, look up the accompanying Scripture references. Under each statement, record your thoughts about how understanding that truth about the Spirit should affect our lives.

a. The Holy Spirit is a Person. He is not an impersonal force or thing. Many people refer to the Spirit as an "it," but the Bible consistently describes the Spirit as a Person (for example, see Matthew 28:19 where the Spirit is an equal member of the personal Godhead or Ephesians 4:30 where He is said to have emotions). Rather than using the Spirit as an energy boost or tapping into Him like an electric current, we actually talk to Him, relate to Him, cooperate with Him, and make ourselves available to Him. Give an example of how this difference between Person and thing should affect the way we live.

b. *The Holy Spirit is God.* He is not less than the Father or the Son; He is consistently presented as equal (Matt. 28:19). Just like the other members of the

Godhead, the Spirit is sometimes referred to simply as "God" (Acts 5:3–4). How do you think this ought to change the way we relate to Him?

c. *The Holy Spirit has His own mind and will.* He thinks and acts according to His own will and the will of God the Father (Rom. 8:27; 1 Cor. 12:11). The Spirit strategically enables and empowers us to fulfill our mission here on earth. How should the thought that the Holy Spirit has His own mind and will affect the way you think and plan?

d. *The Holy Spirit has emotions.* Paul tells us not to grieve the Holy Spirit (Eph. 4:30). When there is disunity and lack of love, whether with other people or with God Himself, we cause the Spirit to grieve. We rarely think about the effect our sin has on God, but He is clearly saddened when we fail to honor Him as we ought. How should understanding that the Spirit can be grieved affect our attitudes toward sin?

e. *The Holy Spirit is all-powerful, all-knowing, and all-present.* In Zechariah 4:6 God calls His people to rely on the power of the Spirit. In 1 Corinthians 2:10, Paul not only says that the Holy Spirit knows everything, but that He reveals truth to us. And in Psalm 139:7–8, David tells us that the Spirit is everywhere, and we cannot escape His presence. How do these three truths affect the way we look to the Spirit?

As you study the Holy Spirit, keep in mind that you shouldn't be trying to fully comprehend Him—you can't! "The point is not to completely understand God but to worship Him" (*Forgotten God*, 65). What you learn about the Holy Spirit should lead you to value Him more and desire His active presence in your life. How is He doing that thus far?

## What the Holy Spirit Does In and Through Us

When Jesus left earth to go back to the Father, He left us, His followers, with an impossible task: "You will be my witnesses in Jerusalem and in all Judea and Samaria, and to the end of the earth" (Acts 1:8). But before sending His disciples out to accomplish that task, He told them to wait: "He ordered them not to depart from Jerusalem, but to wait for the promise of the Father, which, he said, 'you heard from me; for John baptized with water, but you will be baptized with the Holy Spirit not many days from now'" (Acts 1:4–5). And as Jesus sent them out, He was clear that they would need the power of the Spirit: "But you will receive power when the Holy Spirit has come upon you, and you will be my witnesses" (Acts 1:8).

Don't forget that God gave the Holy Spirit to us. It sometimes feels so difficult to be a Christian. How do we live lives that are radically different from the world around us? How do we continue the mission that Jesus began and entrusted to us? The answer is: through the power of the Holy Spirit.

7. God's Spirit works in and through us in a variety of ways to glorify Himself. Below is a list of ways that He does this.[1] For each item, ask yourself, "How is the Spirit working in this way in my everyday life? Or how might He do so?" Jot down a brief answer to this question under each point.

a. The Spirit helps us when we are in precarious situations and need to bear witness (Mark 13:11; Luke 12:12).

b. The Counselor teaches and reminds us of what we need to know and remember. He is our comforter, our advisor, our encourager, and our strength. He guides us in the way we should go (Ps. 143:10; John 14—16; Acts 9:31; 13:2; 15:28; 1 Cor. 2:9–10; 1 John 5:6–8).

---

1     This list is taken from *Forgotten God,* pages 74–76.

c. From the Spirit we receive power to be God's witnesses to the ends of the earth. It is the Spirit who draws people to the gospel, the Spirit who equips us with the strength we need to accomplish God's purposes. The Holy Spirit not only initially draws people to God the Father, but He also draws believers closer to Jesus (Acts 1:8; Rom. 8:26; Eph. 3:16–19).

d. By the power of the Spirit we put to death the misdeeds of the body. The Spirit sets us free from sin, which we cannot get rid of on our own. This is a lifelong process we entered into, in partnership with the Spirit, when we first believed (Rom. 8:2).

e. Through the Spirit we have received adoption as children, which leads us into intimacy with the Father, instead of a relationship based on fear and slavery. The Spirit bears witness to us that we are God's children (Rom. 8:15–16).

f. The Holy Spirit convicts people of sin. He does this both before we initially enter into right relationship with God and as we journey through this life as believers (John 16:7–11; 1 Thess. 1:5).

g. The Spirit brings us life and freedom. Where the Spirit is, there is freedom, not bondage or slavery. In our world that is plagued with death, this is a profound truth that points to real hope (Rom. 8:10–11; 2 Cor. 3:17).

h. By the power of the Holy Spirit we abound with hope because our God is a God of hope, who fills His children with all joy and peace (Rom. 15:13).

i. As members of God's kingdom community, each of us is given a manifestation of the Spirit in our lives for the purpose of the common good. We all have something to offer because of what the Spirit gives to us (1 Cor. 12:7).

j. The fruit of being led by the Spirit of God includes love, joy, peace, patience, kindness, goodness, faithfulness, gentleness, and self-control. These attitudes and actions will characterize our lives as we allow ourselves to be grown and molded by the Spirit. The Spirit is our sanctifier (Gal. 5:22–23; 2 Cor. 3:18).

k. The Holy Spirit helps us in our weakness. When we don't know what to pray for or what to do, He actually intercedes on our behalf. He gives us strength in the midst of uncertainty and asks the Father to work according to His will (Rom. 8:26–27).

**Note: What if I don't see these things in my life?**

The Holy Spirit does incredible things in the lives of His children. But what if you're not seeing His action and power in your life? Don't be discouraged. Remember that it's impossible for you to do these things on your own. That's actually the point—it's impossible for you, and that's why God sent us the Spirit.

Sometimes we expect Him to change every aspect of our lives all at once. But that's rarely the way He works. Most often, He works slowly, teaching us to trust Him and increasingly molding us and using us in greater and greater ways. If you want to see the Spirit working in your life, God tells us to ask Him and He will give us the Spirit (Luke 11:13).

Now that you know more (or have been reminded) about what the Holy Spirit does, there's one very important question that you need to ask: What does the Holy Spirit want *me* to do *right now?* How does He want me to cooperate with Him in His work?

Resist the temptation to stop at learning more facts. And don't let yourself believe in what the Spirit can do *hypothetically* rather than what He can do *in your life.* Now that the power available to you in the Holy Spirit is fresh in your mind, consider what God might want to do *through you.* Where might He want you to go? Who might He want you to talk to or serve? All the power in the world is irrelevant until it's put to use.

8. Take a minute to ponder the amazing power of the Spirit of God. Looking at the situations God has placed you in, what do you think He might be calling you to do through the power of the Spirit?

9. Spend some time in prayer. After looking through these Scriptures about who the Holy Spirit is and what He does, there are bound to be a number of things that you need to begin applying to your life. Ask God to fill you with His Spirit so that the world around you will see His power.

# REFLECTIONS ON ...

## Theology of the Holy Spirit 101

# SESSION 4

# WHY DO YOU WANT HIM?

For more information on the material in this session,
read chapter 4 of the book *Forgotten God.*

It is clear that you want to see the Holy Spirit in your life—you wouldn't have made it this far in the study if you didn't. This is a good thing. The first step in reversing our neglect of the Holy Spirit is desiring to see Him work in and through us. But at this point, there is an important question that has to be asked: Why do you want Him?

We all need to question our motives. We can't simply move on and assume that our hearts are in the right place—what's at stake is too important. Why does it matter so much? Motivation makes all the difference in the world. If we pursue the Spirit out of love for God and people, then the power of God will be clearly displayed, but if we try to use the Spirit for our own purposes, we're only demonstrating our pride. It's the difference between being powerfully used by God and being aggressively opposed by Him (James 4:6).

1. Take a minute or two to write down a few possible motivations for desiring the Holy Spirit—both good and bad.

2. Can you detect hints of any of these motivations in your heart? If so, what do you think causes you to be motivated in that way?

Read Acts 8:9–24. Simon the magician was accustomed to incredible displays of power. He used his magic arts to amaze people and convince them that he was someone great. But when he saw the miracles performed through Philip, he himself was amazed. Clearly Simon knew that something out of the ordinary was happening. When someone who spends his life conjuring up powerful displays is left in awe, something special is going on. He was intrigued by the Holy Spirit, drawn by the incredible power he was witnessing.

3. Think about Simon's response in verses 18–19. Why do you think he wanted the Spirit?

4. Try to transfer this situation to our modern day. What would Simon's motivation look like if it were played out in the American church today?

5. Have you seen any examples of this, whether in the church in general, something you've experienced in the past, or (most importantly) in your own heart? If so, describe those examples.

Peter's response highlights the importance of calling our motives into question. On some level, we might be impressed by Simon's desire for the Spirit: "Wow. He really wants the power of the Spirit in his life! He's even willing to give up his worldly possessions to gain the Holy Spirit!" But Peter swiftly addressed Simon's heart. Simon wasn't satisfied with seeing the Spirit at work; he wanted to be the one who controlled the Spirit's power.

The fact that you want to see the Spirit at work is important, but unless your heart is in the right place, Peter's rebuke should cause you to stop in your tracks. Why do you want the Holy Spirit? Your answer really makes a big difference.

The Holy Spirit works to glorify God (John 16:14), but too often, the people who talk the most about the Spirit are the ones who receive all the glory. There is no hint of what Jesus describes in Matthew 5:16: "Let your light shine before others, so that they may see your good works and give glory to your Father who is in heaven." When God truly shines through us, the supernatural is clearly manifested in us, but God gets all the glory.

6. Have you seen a person accomplish something amazing, yet receive all the glory for himself? What does that look like?

7. Have you seen a person accomplish something amazing, yet all the glory goes to God? What does that look like?

As we observed before, when Jesus returned to His Father, He left the disciples with the task of changing the world. He was very clear that they could not do this on their own. Instead, they were told to wait until God clothed them with power through the Holy Spirit. When the Spirit showed up on the day of Pentecost and empowered the disciples to proclaim the gospel in a host of different languages (Acts 2), He demonstrated that genuine works of the Spirit leave no doubt about who should get the glory. "When the Spirit moved at Pentecost, people knew there was a power present that came from God. That's why they didn't leave saying, 'John is amazing! He learned a new language in a matter of seconds!' They knew it had to be God" (*Forgotten God*, 87).

Our focus in all of this needs to be on God—not on ourselves, not even on the things we can accomplish with His power. Instead of deciding in advance what sort of supernatural display God should provide, we should simply ask God to work powerfully in our life situations and allow Him to work in the way He wants.

Sometimes we fixate on the really flashy manifestations of the Spirit, but when a proud person exhibits humility, is this any less supernatural? When a person patiently loves and prays for a grouchy neighbor or coworker for years with no results, does this not show the Spirit's power?

8. List a few of these "less glamorous" ways that the Spirit's power can be manifest in a person's life.

9. Why should these things be seen as powerful manifestations of the Spirit?

Another trap we could easily fall into is trying to lead the Spirit rather than being led by Him. The distinction is sometimes subtle, because in both cases we're seeking the Spirit. But when we go down this path, we start with our own dreams and desires, and we ask for the Spirit to work so that we can accomplish our plans. In this case, we're really following in the footsteps of Simon the magician—he earnestly desired the Spirit, but he wasn't seeking to be led by Him.

10. Practically, what does it look like to be led by the Spirit rather than trying to lead the Spirit for your purposes?

We have to prayerfully seek where the Holy Spirit may be leading. I am convinced that the Spirit communicates with us. Sometimes He lays a person or place on our hearts and calls us to action or prayer. Other times He convicts us of our sin and calls us to repent. He works in many different ways, but the point is, many times we don't hear because we're not listening. Sometimes we hear, but we write it off as nothing because we don't agree with where He's leading.

11. Being completely honest—do you really want to follow the Spirit, regardless of where He may lead you? Why, or why not?

Now that we've addressed a few wrong motivations for desiring the Spirit, we still have to answer an important question: What is the right reason for desiring the Spirit?

Read 1 Corinthians 12:4–11.

According to Paul, the Spirit works in individual lives "for the common good" (v. 7). First Corinthians 12—14 describes the proper function of the church. God has placed each of us in a specific location. Our task is to build up the Christians around us and reach out to the rest of the world. It is actually the Spirit who empowers us to fulfill this calling by giving us supernatural abilities. The flashiest of these are things like prophecy and speaking in tongues, but we shouldn't overlook the fact that encouragement and service are also miraculous manifestations of the Holy Spirit.

Once again, our tendency can be to focus on the specific manifestations of the Spirit that Paul mentions. But even in the midst of describing how the Spirit works through us in these ways, Paul says, "I will show you a still more excellent way" (1 Cor. 12:31). As he describes in chapter 13, that more excellent way is love.

The proper motivation for desiring the Holy Spirit is love for the people that God has placed in our lives. The Spirit works in us because He loves the people around us. Do you love the people in your life enough to pursue the Spirit for their benefit?

12. Describe the difference between someone who pursues the Spirit for their own sake and someone who does so out of love for other people.

If you have the *Forgotten God DVD Study Resource,* watch the video for session 4, particularly if you are meeting with a group. After the video, come back and work through the rest of this section.

If we're going to be open for the Holy Spirit to work in our lives, we must first let go of the things that keep us from close fellowship with Him. The Spirit works through each of us so that we can build up the people around us in love. Having the Holy Spirit is not about you being everything you want to be. It's about God working through you to help the people around you grow.

Do you trust that God can speak to you through the people He has placed in your life? Does your desire for the Spirit include openness to the Spirit leading someone else to honestly speak truth into your life? Are you willing to follow the Spirit's leading in being honest with the people around you?

If the proper motivation for desiring the Spirit is love, ask yourself how much you love the people around you. Sometimes the most loving thing you can do is speak gently and honestly into another person's life.

13. Spend some time in prayer. Ask God for the humility and love to speak honestly into the lives of the people around you. And as other people are honest with you, ask the Spirit to work in your heart, removing the sinful thoughts and motivations and allowing you to grow and follow the Spirit for the benefit of those around you.

# REFLECTIONS ON ...

## Why Do You Want Him?

**SESSION 5**

# A REAL RELATIONSHIP

For more information on the material in this session,
read chapter 5 of the book *Forgotten God.*

What comes to mind when you think about relationships? Do you think of having long conversations? Spending time with someone? Going out of your way to make someone happy? Maybe your mind goes straight to a specific person and how much he or she means to you.

Or perhaps your view of relationships isn't so warm and cozy. Maybe every time you've opened your heart and life to someone you've been disappointed and burned. If that's the case, the thought of relationships might be associated with insecurity.

When it comes to a relationship with God, there is nothing worse than insecurity and nothing better than enjoying an ongoing intimacy and confidence in your relationship.

1. Before you go any further, honestly describe your relationship with God. Be descriptive—how does your relationship feel, how do you maintain it, and so on?

*I'm negligent.*

Most believers understand that Christianity is about a relationship with God. But we don't always recognize the Spirit's critical role in that relationship.

Read Galatians 4:1–7.

In the book of Galatians, Paul teaches about the role of the Law for the Jewish people in the Old Testament. He says that the Law was given to watch over and guide the nation of Israel until Jesus Christ, the Messiah, came to set them free. In order to explain this, Paul contrasts two types of people: slaves and sons.

2. Think about this imagery. What is the difference between a slave and a son? List some differences between the two. (For example, what treatment does each receive? What privileges does each have? How does each feel? What confidence does each have?)

| Slaves | Sons |
| --- | --- |
| fear insecurity shame | embraced forgiven gifts-Holy spirit His presence |

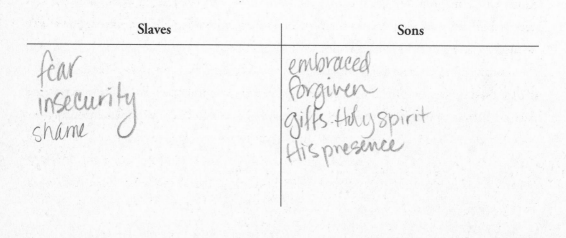

The incredible truth is that in Christ we have been adopted by God. Whether or not we feel like children of God, this is reality. But God wasn't satisfied with simply adopting us; He wanted to be sure that we would *feel* like children of God. Paul says that God gave us the Holy Spirit for that very reason: "Because you are sons, God has sent the Spirit of his Son into our hearts, crying, 'Abba! Father!'" (Gal. 4:6).

That term "Abba" was the most endearing way to address a father. The modern equivalent would be the word "Daddy." Let the significance of this hit you. It's incredible enough that we can call almighty God our Father. But then He sends the Holy Spirit into our hearts and prompts us to cry out to Him, "Daddy!"

3. What is the significance of Paul's statement here? How should it affect your relationship with God to know that He sent the Holy Spirit into your heart to cry out "Abba!"?

*He is our father. He wants us to feel love & comforted. We are his children*

Read Romans 8:12–17. In this passage, Paul makes basically the same statement. We have it confirmed once again—the Holy Spirit lives within us in order to convince us that we are God's children: "You did not receive the spirit of slavery to fall back into fear, but you have received the Spirit of adoption as sons, by whom we cry, 'Abba! Father!' The Spirit himself bears witness with our spirit that we are children of God" (Rom. 8:15–16).

In this case, Paul adds the thought that we should not fall back into fear as though we were slaves. Because we are not yet perfected, we all sin on a regular basis. For many of us, falling into sin can cause us insecurity in our relationship with God. We begin to feel unworthy and afraid. Our response is just like that of the Prodigal Son. In shame, he crawled back to the father, believing that he could not be accepted as a son, but hoping that he might be able to serve as a slave. Imagine his shock and overwhelming joy when the father came running to embrace him as a son!

4. Most of us experience situations where our guilt or perfectionism keeps us from enjoying intimacy with God. In times like these, how should the truth of Romans 8:15–17 restore our intimacy with God?

*We need to run to Him + embrace Abba father & Holy Spirit.*

How do you feel about the truth?

*Hard to believe someone - especially God could love me like that.*
*fellowship, relationship w/ Him*

**(DVD)** If you have the *Forgotten God DVD Study Resource*, watch the video for session 5, particularly if you are meeting with a group. After the video, come back and work through the rest of this section.

Though we don't always realize it, intimacy with God is the deepest desire of the human heart. Not only that, but God also strongly desires a relationship with us—so much so that He sent His Spirit into our hearts so that we could have constant fellowship with Him.

To some extent, we all know what it's like to feel close to another person, whether it be a mom or dad, a husband or wife, a child, a sibling, or just a good friend. Whatever it is, there's nothing like sharing a close personal relationship.

5. Most of us tend to take our relationships for granted, but what is it that makes
   close personal relationships so incredible?

No matter how close you may feel with another human being, the potential for intimacy with
the Holy Spirit is always greater. Close friends may stick by your side no matter what, but the
Holy Spirit actually lives inside of you! Think about it, every second of every day the Spirit of
the living God is within you—"Where shall I go from your Spirit? Or where shall I flee from
your presence?" (Ps. 139:7).

At this point, most of us start to wonder, "If this is true, why don't I feel close to Him?" I
think that most of us become distanced from the Spirit for two primary reasons: comfort and
noise.

In John 14, Jesus refers to the Holy Spirit as the "Helper" or "Comforter" (KJV). Though
it is a reassuring thought to have a Helper and Comforter on hand, many of us have made our
lives so comfortable and "safe" that we don't need to be comforted. Usually, it's not until an
unexpected tragedy strikes that we feel uncomfortable.

6. Have you ever found yourself in a place where you absolutely needed the
   Spirit to help or comfort you? If so, what was it like and how did the Spirit
   comfort you?

7. If you answered no to that question (or if you had to think about it awhile), do you think you should consider living a more radical life where you need the Spirit to come through? Why, or why not?

*I avoid people-certain ones-due to drama*

If your life isn't too comfortable, it's probably too noisy. One of the most observed and bemoaned aspects of life in the twenty-first century is the rapid pace of everything. When we're not busy at work, we're on the phone or talking to friends and family. Even inanimate objects demand our attention—televisions, iPods, radios, newspapers, computers, books (like this one), and so on.

8. When was the last time you sat quietly with nothing at all to distract you? What was that like?

You may need to do something about this right now. Your life may have become so busy and so noisy that you haven't sat alone with God for weeks—maybe even years. Maybe taking the time to go through this workbook is yet another distraction that is keeping you from intimacy with God. If that's the case, set it aside and spend some time speaking and listening to God directly. You absolutely won't regret it.

9. List some of the things that distract you from a real relationship with God.

10. Which of those things do you need to get rid of or back off on in order to
    pursue intimacy with God? How can you do this?

I hope this section doesn't come across as harsh or accusing. You may have an incredible relationship with God. Maybe He's more real to you than the people around you. If that's true, then praise God! That's the goal we're all headed toward. My purpose in writing this is to help you maintain that relationship through the power of the Spirit and to remove some of the things that inhibit intimacy with God.

The most important reason to pursue a relationship with the Spirit of God is that Jesus gave His life so that you could pursue one. As Paul explained, "Christ redeemed us from the curse of the law by becoming a curse for us … so that we might receive the promised Spirit through faith" (Gal. 3:13–14).

At times, you may be tempted to feel that the Spirit is keeping Himself distant from you or that you're trying to find God, but He doesn't want to be found. When that thought enters your mind, remember the truth of Galatians 3:14. Jesus died so that you could receive the Spirit. He purchased that intimacy for you at the greatest possible price.

11. Are you guilty of taking the Holy Spirit for granted? If so, how can you begin to reverse that trend in your life?

Remember that it is the Holy Spirit who cries out, "Abba! Father!" in your heart. He is the one who bears witness with your spirit that you are a child of God. God has adopted you into His family. May you be empowered by the Holy Spirit to approach Him as your Daddy. May you stand secure in your relationship with Him, and may that overflow into the intimacy that comes through obediently walking in the Spirit.

12. Spend some time in prayer. Ask God to draw you closer to Himself. Pray that His Holy Spirit would increase your intimacy as a child of the living God.

# REFLECTIONS ON ...

## A Real Relationship

SESSION 6

# FORGET ABOUT HIS WILL FOR YOUR LIFE!

For more information on the material in this session,
read chapter 6 of the book *Forgotten God.*

What are you going to accomplish with your life? That's a big question; maybe we can break it down into something a little easier: What's your five-year plan? Maybe you can answer that question, no problem. Or maybe you feel sick to your stomach when you have to make plans for the weekend.

Probably the most-asked question at graduations is, "What are you going to do with your life?" For whatever reason, we tend to focus on what we can and should do in the future, rather than what we can and should do today.

This often bleeds over into our relationship with God. Most of the college students I have counseled have a common problem: "I want to follow God, but I just can't figure out His will for my life." This can be such a huge preoccupation that they don't consider what God wants them to do right now, in the situations that He has placed them in at this moment.

1. Why might it be safer to commit to following "God's will for your life" rather than following God in what He may lead you to do today?

There's nothing wrong with pursuing what God would have you do with your life, but sometimes we get so scared about missing our calling for the future that we become paralyzed in the present. God does have a plan for each of our lives, but He has never promised to reveal that plan to us in advance.

**If you have the *Forgotten God DVD Study Resource,* watch the video for session 6, particularly if you are meeting with a group. After the video, come back and work through the rest of this section.**

2. The video poses an important question: If you were absolutely, 100 percent submitted to the will of God at this moment, what do you think He might ask you to do?

The moment you heard that question, maybe you knew exactly what God would want you to do. He's been calling you to it for a long time, but you've been writing it off as anything but the voice of God. If that's the case, consider leaving this study and following the Spirit in whatever He's leading you to do. Don't let this workbook be one more thing that keeps you from obeying the voice of God.

However, that may be a tough question for you to answer. You may have no idea what God "might" call you to. But that's not really the point. Generally speaking, the answer is not as important as the question. Daily considering and pursuing the Spirit's leading in our lives is crucial.

Read Romans 8:1–13.

In Romans 7, Paul discusses the impossibility of obedience in the flesh: "I have the desire to do what is right, but not the ability to carry it out" (v. 18). This is a hopeless situation. But what is impossible in Romans 7 is made possible in Romans 8. What makes the difference? The Holy Spirit.

"The Spirit of life has set you free in Christ Jesus from the law of sin and death" (8:2). According to Romans 8, the difference between trying and failing, and truly obeying God has everything to do with following the Spirit's leading.

3. In verses 5–8, Paul talks about the difference between the mind set on the flesh and the mind set on the Spirit. Think about this difference. Give an example of what each type of person looks like.

4. Look at verses 9–13. What things does Paul mention that set the Spirit-filled person apart?

5. What do you think it means to "by the Spirit you put to death the deeds of the body" (v. 13)?

Paul refers to this process of following the Spirit's leading as walking "according to the Spirit" in Romans 8:4 and walking "by the Spirit" in Galatians 5:16 and 25. The concept of walking is so basic that perhaps you've never considered what walking entails. Think about how simple it is: You don't have to know exactly where you're going; it doesn't require any planning; all you have to do is put one foot in front of the other. Really, the only way to walk is one step at a time.

We can get so caught up in the big picture that we lose sight of the fact that God is simply calling us to walk. It won't necessarily be easy, but we can always put one foot in front of the other.

6. Think about the analogy of walking. Practically, what would it mean for you to walk by the Spirit in your daily life?

When we walk by the Spirit, we are moving in a particular direction, and that direction is set by the Spirit. As we discussed in session 4, our motivation in desiring the Spirit is important. Walking by the Spirit is not about adding the Spirit into your already busy life:

> The Spirit who raised Christ from the dead is not someone
> we can just call on when we want a little extra power in our
> lives. Jesus Christ did not die in order to follow *us*. He died
> and rose again so that we could forget everything else and
> follow Him to the cross, to true Life. (*Forgotten God,* 122)

There is a real difference between adding the Spirit to your life and actually following Him minute by minute. If you add the Spirit to your life, you're not open to change; you just want to enhance what you're already doing. This is not what the Spirit came to do.

On the other hand, if you begin following the Spirit's leading in your life, you will find yourself changing. The Spirit may prompt you to let go of things that were once important to you. He may even call you to give up some good things in your life, at least for a time, in order to accomplish His purposes in and through you.

7. The thought of being called to give things up may be scary, but honestly answer this question: Which is more frightening to you, giving up everything you own, or going through life on your own without the Holy Spirit? Why do you say that?

I don't mean to give the impression that you always have to choose between the two. But it's an important question to ask yourself, because anything that you value more than God is an idol. The rich young ruler in Mark 10:17–22 didn't realize what was keeping him from God until Jesus asked him a similar question. By definition, submitting to the Spirit's leading means giving up control.

Sometimes we get the impression that being Spirit-filled doesn't require continued action. It's important to recognize that being filled with the Spirit is not a one-time act. When we put our faith in Christ, the Holy Spirit begins living within us, and we are sealed in Him (Eph. 1:13). That will never change. Yet even those who have received the Spirit of God are called to be filled with the Spirit (Eph. 5:18).

Being filled with the Spirit is really a lifelong process. The Holy Spirit will be working in us continually until the day we leave this earth: "And we all, with unveiled face, beholding the glory of the Lord, are being transformed into the same image from one degree of glory to another. For this comes from the Lord who is the Spirit" (2 Cor. 3:18). The implication is that this is not an event; it's an ongoing relationship in which the Spirit continues to work in us to make us the people He wants us to be.

8. Though we might wish that being Spirit-filled were as easy as an event, what are the benefits of maintaining an ongoing relationship with the Holy Spirit?

Walking by the Spirit comes down to daily dependence on God. Sometimes the struggle with sin seems hopeless, but remember that if you are actively walking in the Spirit, you won't sin (Gal. 5:16). This doesn't necessarily mean that your struggle with sin will get easier, but it does provide hope. You may find a particular sin difficult to resist, but as you become more sensitive to the Spirit's leading, you will begin doing the things that He leads you to do. He will never lead you into sin, so anytime you fall into sin, you are disregarding the Spirit's leading in your life. I'm not claiming that it will suddenly be easy, but as you begin following the Spirit's leading more and more, you will see sin in your life less and less.

9. Identify a particular sin in your life. What would it look like to be Spirit-led in a moment of temptation? (If you're working with a small group, you won't be asked to name the specific sin unless you feel it would be beneficial for the group.)

We all know people who are daily walking by the Spirit. These people are actively maintaining their relationship with God and constantly opening themselves to follow the Spirit's leading, whatever that may mean. The most difficult part is the daily maintenance.

Most of us are excited about submitting to the Spirit in an abstract sense. We enjoy the thought of being filled with the Spirit. But how often do you consider the way the Spirit might be leading as you spend time with your family? What might the Spirit want you to say to the people you work with? Have you thought about how the Spirit might want you to shape your budget? These are all practical areas that we rarely consider submitting to the Spirit.

10. Think about some of these mundane daily activities. In which of these are you prone to do your own thing without considering how the Spirit might lead you?

11. How can you turn these activities into opportunities to follow the Spirit's leading?

As we discuss the Spirit-filled life, there can be a real pressure to try harder in our own strength to produce the "fruit of the Spirit" mentioned in Galatians 5:22–23. Maybe studying the Holy Spirit has made you feel even more overwhelmed, like you'll never be the kind of person that God wants you to be. If that's the case, then you're not seeing an important truth: *All of this life-change and obedience comes through the power of the Spirit.*

Everything we've been discussing could sound exhausting, but we have to remember that God is not calling us to do this in our own strength. Certainly the Spirit guides and directs us, but it's vital to remember that He also empowers us. Paul rebuked the Galatian churches for trying to grow in their own strength: "Are you so foolish? Having begun by the Spirit, are you now being perfected by the flesh?" (Gal. 3:3). And though it's a confusing thought, He actually called the Philippians to actively work *because* God was working in them (Phil. 2:12–13). I don't know exactly how it all fits together, but as we follow the Spirit's leading in our lives, He also provides the strength and power to walk.

12. We have a tendency to try to do the Spirit's work in our own strength. Practically, how can you do the work of the Spirit through the power of the Spirit?

13. Spend some time in prayer. Ask God what He wants you to do—not in five years, but right now, today. Pray for strength to follow the Spirit's leading in whatever He may be calling you to do.

# REFLECTIONS ON ...

## Forget About His Will for Your Life!

# SESSION 7

# SUPERNATURAL CHURCH

For more information on the material in this session,
read chapter 7 of the book *Forgotten God.*

Unfortunately, one of the most striking similarities that most churchgoers share with the non-Christian world is their ability to complain about the way the church operates. We all do it from time to time. But think positively for a minute:

1. If you could create the perfect church, what would it look like? (How would it be run? How would people act, reach out, worship, pray, and so on?)

Now consider this question: Could that perfect church be accomplished through human talent and strength? Or would it require the power of the Holy Spirit? Why?

Let's be honest: We could duplicate most of our successful churches by assembling the right group of talented, winsome people. If a church has the right worship leader, an exciting children's program, and an entertaining speaker, it will grow. But is that really the secret to life-changing ministry? Is that how God designed the church to operate? Where does the Holy Spirit fit in that model? As much as I believe in using our natural abilities for God's glory, I simply cannot reconcile that model with the Lord's statement: "Not by might, nor by power, but by my Spirit, says the LORD of hosts" (Zech. 4:6).

All of our natural talents come from God, and I'm not trying to downplay using your unique gifts and abilities. But if our lives and churches make perfect sense in light of human talent and strength, then something is missing: "I don't want my life to be explainable without the Holy Spirit. I want people to look at my life and know that I couldn't be doing this by my own power. I want to live in such a way that I am desperate for Him to come through" (*Forgotten God*, 142).

2. Consider your involvement with church life. In what ways do we tend to rely on natural talent as we strive to fulfill the church's mission?

If you have the *Forgotten God DVD Study Resource,* watch the video for session 7, particularly if you are meeting with a group. After the video, come back and work through the rest of this section.

The cartoon in the video gives a powerful illustration of the church today: We get excited about the tractor, then wear ourselves out pushing it inch by inch through the field. At the end of the harvest, we've barely managed to finish the job and end up with just enough food to go around. Tragically, this is how many churches operate—they are built on the sweat and effort of a few talented (but exhausted) leaders.

When we consult the owner's manual, however, we find that the tractor is actually designed to run and plow the field on its own. So we fix the tractor, plow the field in a single night, and then share the overabundance of food with everyone in need. When we discover that the church was designed to function through the power of the Holy Spirit, it changes everything.

3. Think about the tractor illustration. Do you see yourself and/or your church pushing and pulling the "tractor" an inch at a time? If so, in what ways?

Read 1 Corinthians 1:26—2:5.

When Paul wrote his first letter to the church in Corinth, he had to address factions that were dividing the church. Groups were forming around attractive personalities (Paul, Apollos, Cephas). In order to address their preoccupation with human personalities and wisdom, Paul brought their focus back to the power of God, rather than the brilliance of men.

4. How does Paul describe human effort as compared to the power of God?

5. According to this passage, why is it so important to rely on the power of the Spirit? (See especially 2:5.)

6. Think about the way you minister to the people around you. Can you say along with Paul, "My speech and my message were not in plausible words of wisdom, but in demonstration of the Spirit and of power, that your faith might not rest in the wisdom of men but in the power of God" (1 Cor. 2:4–5)? Why, or why not?

What's true of the church in general is also true of our lives in particular. There ought to be a real difference between a Spirit-filled person and everyone else. I'm not necessarily talking about walking around raising the dead and speaking foreign languages all the time.

Remember the fruit of the Spirit in Galatians 5? The fruit mentioned there is not all that shocking. Many non-Christians are actually happy, peaceful people.

But as Christians, we have the Source of both joy and peace *living inside of us*. So while anyone can show love at times and to certain extents, we who have the Holy Spirit ought to love the people around us to a supernatural degree in any and every circumstance. Sometimes the difference isn't apparent until tragedy strikes. When we find ourselves in the midst of overwhelming circumstances, the Spirit has a chance to show His incredible power.

7. Have you ever witnessed a person manifesting the fruit of the Spirit to a supernatural degree? How did God show His power through that person?

The Spirit wants to do more than just help us out a bit. He wants to transform us, patiently but steadily, into people who transform our corners of the world. We sometimes get so caught up in everything God wants us to *do* that we lose sight of who God wants us to *be*. The difference is significant. God wants us to be the type of people who love Him wholeheartedly, who depend on the Holy Spirit, who by faith reach out to the people around us. As we spend time pursuing God and enjoying fellowship with the Spirit, we will begin to see our lives changing from the inside out.

We won't be transformed by simply trying harder. "Grunting and saying through clenched teeth, 'I *will* be patient!' hasn't worked yet, and that isn't likely to change. But what does effect change is when we begin to ask God to make these fruit manifest in our lives, by the power of His Spirit, and when we spend time in communion with our God" (*Forgotten God*, 148–149). Remember, it's never been about you doing it on your own. It's about the power of the Spirit in your life.

8. What would it look like for you to cultivate a relationship with the Spirit, allowing Him to transform you, rather than simply trying harder on your own?

It's been brought up in previous chapters, but perhaps we don't recognize the Spirit's power in our lives because we're not stepping out and doing anything where we desperately need God to show up. Anyone can show up to a Sunday meeting, sing a few songs, sit still for forty-five minutes, shake a few hands, and then drive home.

But when you start talking to the hurting people around you, digging deeper to learn how you can love and serve them, that's when you need the Holy Spirit, and that's precisely when He shows up! God works in the most desperate situations so that no one can mistake it for anything other than His power. Maybe He will grant you boldness to speak in a frightening situation. Maybe He will give you a divine compassion for the lost and destitute. Maybe He will give you the wisdom to say exactly what a person needs to hear at a crucial moment in his or her life. You won't know what God will do until you get out there and follow His leading. The question is, do you trust Him enough to follow Him into the unknown, confident that He will work powerfully in that situation?

We absolutely need to step beyond our own abilities. It's much safer to stay where we're comfortable, but our lack of confidence in God's power does not bring Him any glory. You get praised for using your natural talents well. God gets praised when His power accomplishes the humanly impossible.

9. Have you ever walked away from a ministry opportunity because it would take you beyond your natural talents? In what areas would you need the Spirit to empower you in a situation like that?

10. Do you believe that the Spirit would "come through" for you in that type of situation? Why, or why not?

Throughout these seven sessions you've thought through the importance of the Holy Spirit from a number of different angles. We could always study more, but it's time to act (if you haven't already). This is by far the most difficult part. It's time to follow the Spirit's leading, even if you're not sure where He's taking you or how you'll get through it. The world desperately needs to see a united church that is absolutely submitted to and filled with the Holy Spirit.

11. Allow yourself to dream for a minute. What would it look like if every Christian in your community fully submitted themselves to the Spirit's leading?

12. What practical steps can you take right now to pursue the Spirit and live in dependence on Him?

It all comes down to one important question: Will you rely on your natural abilities, or will you allow the Holy Spirit to use you in incredible ways? The way you proceed will determine if you as an individual and your church as a group of individuals will be stoppable or unstoppable.

If you rely on our own talents, you can be stopped so easily. You could get tired, distracted, overwhelmed, attacked. But if the Holy Spirit moves through His church, nothing can stand in the way. Rather than the weak, this-worldly churches we're so familiar with, the church would actually look like Jesus said it would: "I will build my church, and the gates of hell shall not prevail against it" (Matt. 16:18). I believe that God will empower His church in this way, but the question is, do we want Him to start with us?

13. As we end this study, spend more time than usual in prayer. Pray that the Spirit of God would radically transform your life from the inside out. Pray that your life will never be the same.

# REFLECTIONS ON ...

## Supernatural Church

# NOTES FOR DISCUSSION LEADERS

A small group working through this material will benefit from having a discussion leader. If that's you, don't worry—you don't need to have all the answers. After all, when we study God, we're not going to understand Him fully. But we can get to know Him better and respond in worship. Also, this workbook is discussion-driven, not teacher-driven. All you need is the willingness to prepare each week, guide the discussion, and rely on the Holy Spirit to work in your heart and the hearts of group members. This study can give you a hands-on experience of depending not on your natural leadership abilities but on the Spirit. If you pray for His help, He will give it.

## Discussion Leader's Job Description

The discussion leader's job isn't to have all the answers. He or she simply needs to:

- Keep the group on track when it's tempted to go off on a tangent.

- Keep the discussion moving so that it doesn't get stuck on one question.

- Make sure that everyone gets a chance to talk and that no one dominates (it is not necessary that every person respond aloud to every question, but every person should have the chance to do so).

- Make sure that the discussion remains respectful.

## Preparing for the Discussion

As the discussion leader, you'll probably want to read the chapters from the book *Forgotten God* before each session. If you can view the video ahead of time, that's great. Try to work through your own responses to the discussion questions ahead of time as well. Just before the meeting, be sure the chairs are arranged so that everyone can see one another.

## Guiding the Discussion

A few ground rules can make the discussion deeper:

- *Confidentiality:* Whatever is said in the group stays in the group. Nothing is to be repeated to those who weren't there.

- *Honesty:* We're not here to impress each other. We're here to grow and to know each other.

- *Respect:* Disagreement is welcome. Disrespect is not.

The discussion should be a conversation among the group members, not a one-on-one with the leader. You can encourage this with statements like, "Thanks, Allison. What do others of you think?" or "Does anyone have a similar experience, or a different one?"

Don't be afraid of silence—it means group members are thinking about how to answer a question. Trust the Spirit, and wait. Sometimes it's helpful to rephrase the question in your own words. Then wait for others' responses, and avoid jumping in with your own.

I recommend discussing the numbered questions in order. Read each question aloud and ask the group to respond. Even if an answer seems obvious, have a few people share their thoughts—you never know what will spark a challenging conversation.

If you have a copy of the *Forgotten God DVD Study Resource* (I definitely recommend this for groups), stop and watch the appropriate video when prompted. After the video, work through the remaining questions. Feel free to read a section out loud if the group is unclear on what a question is getting at. There is also a segment at the end of this section that contains explanatory notes for discussion leaders. I recommend looking these up before your group meets.

I considered including a section with answers to the questions to help you in leading the discussion. Ultimately, I decided against it, because the most profitable aspect of studying this material in a group is the discussion itself. The destination is important, but you can't get there without the journey. Where specific answers are required, I've tried to point you toward the Scriptures. The answer may not always jump out at you, but at the very least your discussion will be headed in the right direction.

The answers are important, but I am most concerned that people may study the Holy Spirit and never *know* Him, never be *changed* by Him. With every session, keep asking yourself and your group: "How should this change us? If we really submitted our lives to the Holy Spirit and opened ourselves up to His power, what would He have us do, where would He have us go?" At the end of the day, it's about laying hold of the power of the Spirit in order to accomplish what God has placed us on this earth to do. It's about advancing the kingdom of God. It's about His will being done on earth as in heaven.

Most of all, spend time praying for your group. You can't talk anyone into being filled with the Spirit. Pray that the Spirit of God would fill your lives and do the impossible in and through you. In the book of Acts, the human actors were just ordinary, weak people, but the Holy Spirit accomplished unbelievable things through these ordinary people as they prayed and submitted themselves to following His leading. May that be the case with your group as you seek to remember the forgotten God.

# Session 1

*Question 3.* You'll have to decide how you want to handle this question when you meet. If group members have looked up passages on their own before the group meeting, you could skip to question 4 and ask what they would expect of the Spirit in light of these passages. Or you might want to have each member look up a passage or two, read these to the rest of the group, and summarize what they reveal about the Spirit.

*Question 5.* Try to keep the group from being overly negative about specific people in your church. Either keep the discussion a little more general ("Why do our lives tend not to match the biblical descriptions?") or a little more introspective ("Why doesn't my life match the biblical descriptions?"). The point is to help your group think through the disconnect between the New Testament and our experience today.

*Question 6.* You're not necessarily looking for a single right answer here, but try to focus on the things that Paul mentions in this passage (for example, not gratifying the desires of the flesh, or being patient and kind).

*Question 8.* For example, going to church every Sunday, being a nice person, serving every week as an usher or worship leader.

*Question 9.* The answers to this question may be the same as in question 8, but they will be true to a supernatural degree. For example, anyone can be nice, but if the Holy Spirit works in someone's life, that person will be joyful and self-sacrificing to a supernatural degree.

*Question 11.* If some group members answer in the negative, thank them for their honesty. You don't need to convince them that they need to change at this point. Instead, help them identify some reasons for not wanting to change. For instance, maybe they like life as is, or they enjoy a particular sin too much.

# Session 2

*Question 3.* Use this question as a means of finding out where everyone is. Don't let group members argue or try to persuade each other to switch camps. The important thing is for each person to understand what background, baggage, and assumptions he or she brings to the table.

*Question 4.* Avoid lecturing those who answer negatively. Thank them for their honesty and consider praying for their specific fears at the end of your time together.

*Question 7.* Obviously this is just speculation, but it's important for us to try to identify with the ruler, placing ourselves in his shoes, so to speak.

*Question 10.* If group members answer in the negative, thank them for their honesty. Ask if anyone else identifies with their uncertainty and then pray for the ability to follow the Spirit at the end of your time together.

*Question 11.* If group members have written answers ahead of time, you may decide not to ask them to share answers with the group. But if you think it would be beneficial to address together, try asking if anyone would like to share what he or she wrote. If your group is open with one another, this could be a great time of confessing and repenting of sin. But don't be discouraged if no one wants to share. If group members have not written answers ahead of time, encourage them to do this on their own after the meeting.

# Session 3

*Question 6.* Depending on how much time you have and whether group members have prepared on their own, you might want to assign a statement or two to each person. Give people a few minutes to process their sections. Once everyone has formulated a few thoughts, ask each person to read his or her section out loud and share a few thoughts with the group.

On the other hand, if group members have written their answers ahead of time, they may be quicker to process what they would like to share.

*Question 7.* If you have time, walk through this list and discuss how each of these could play out in your everyday lives. If you're running short on time, consider using this section as a prayer time. Spend a few minutes in prayer, and have different group members pray that the Spirit would manifest Himself in some of the ways described in the list.

# Session 4

*Question 3.* Try to place the group in Simon's shoes. What must it have been like to be a magician before the rise of modern science and the growing skepticism of the supernatural? What would it have been like to have people think you were something great on a regular basis? How might a person like that react when presented with an even greater power?

*Question 4.* Based on the motivations your group identified in question 3, how would those motivations for desiring the Spirit play out in a modern church setting? Obviously, your answers here will be subjective and speculative.

*Question 5.* With this question and the next, make sure your group doesn't begin to gossip about people in your church. The point is to get a feel for how these wrong motivations play out so that we can avoid them ourselves.

*Question 8.* For example, a woman who is joyful amid the suffering of having her husband divorcing her, or a young person who encourages the people around him to a supernatural degree.

*Question 11.* If group members answer negatively, thank them for their honesty, and try to identify with their doubts. They don't have to have it all figured out yet, and it's better to be honest at this point and learn to grow together with the rest of the group.

*Question 13.* As a group, I encourage you to begin this process right now. Start by praying for humility and love. Then ask the people around you to speak gently, lovingly, and honestly to you in order to help you grow. This won't be easy, but if you want to grow, this is an important part of the process. As a discussion leader, try to be sensitive to the people in your group. Not everyone handles critique in the same way. Some people like to be hit in the face with the truth; others need a more gentle approach. Don't be afraid to change the activity or stop and pray if you feel that the exercise is too much for some of the members of your group.

## Session 5

*Question 6.* If no one in your group has any examples of this, try thinking through your favorite Bible stories. Joseph was imprisoned on false charges; Ruth was widowed and all but hopeless because she decided to stay with her mother-in-law; Daniel was thrown into the lions' den for praying to God; Paul and Silas were imprisoned for preaching the gospel. In each of these cases, these godly men and women absolutely needed God's power and comfort. Bringing up some of these stories could help the group think about what it means to truly *need* the Spirit.

*Question 10.* The point of this question is not to get rid of every staple of the Information Age, but to consider limiting or removing those things that keep us so distracted that we never spend time with God. Maybe the answer is not to get rid of any devices, but to re-budget your time.

*Question 11.* You don't have to solve this issue once and for all at this point. But hopefully your group has gained enough insight into the Spirit by now to start making suggestions about how to pursue the Spirit. Also, don't underestimate "obvious" answers like "pray more" or "continue getting to know the Spirit by reading the Scriptures."

## Session 6

*Question 2.* Your group may respond by saying, "I have never sensed God asking me to do anything." If that's the case, push back by asking them what things God has told them *in the Bible* that He wants them to do. For example, God wants you to love your neighbor, to care for the poor, to serve the people around you, to proclaim the good news of Jesus Christ. If you know you ought to be doing these things and you're not doing them, then what does God want you to do?

*Question 9.* Not only are some sins difficult to discuss, but some things are not beneficial to talk through in a group setting, especially in mixed-gender groups. Consider giving group members a chance to share their answer if they want to, but don't require every person to share. Instead, think of a few hypothetical situations that the group could discuss. For example, "Let's say your spouse just snapped at you, and you're strongly tempted to respond in anger. What would it look like to be Spirit-led in that situation?"

*Question 11.* This type of question is highly subjective. The point is not to arrive at a definitive answer but to discuss possible ways to open our daily lives to the Spirit's leading. There probably is no easy answer, but if your group starts viewing everyday activities as opportunities to be led by the Spirit, you're on the right track.

*Question 12.* Again, this is a difficult question to answer, and the point is to think it through, not necessarily to decide on an answer. What I really want your group members to think through is how to rely on the Spirit. For instance, one simple thing a person can do is just cultivate the habit of asking, "Lord, what would You like me to do here?" or "Lord, please give me the courage to follow through here."

## Session 7

*Question 2.* With this question I'm thinking of doing good, biblical activities, but relying on our abilities rather than the Spirit's empowerment. For example, using your skills of persuasion to write a clever sermon, but never asking the Spirit to guide you or empower the church to obey what is preached. Or using your people skills to be friendly as a greeter, but never asking the Spirit to supernaturally fill you with joy and compassion for the people you'll greet.

*Question 4.* Make sure the discussion doesn't promote passive or lazy service to God. Paul's point in this passage is that we shouldn't rely on or be enamored with human ingenuity. Basically, Paul isn't downplaying our effort; he's urging the Corinthians to put their faith and confidence in God's power, not man's.

*Question 8.* For a question like this, don't overlook the "obvious" answers: pray more, read the Bible, and so on. The point is, we can't just try harder to be joyful. Instead, we should develop a relationship with the Spirit by praying to Him, asking Him to guide us, reading about Him in the Scriptures, and worshipping Him based on what we know of Him. As we draw closer to Him, His fruit will begin to manifest itself in our lives.

*Question 9.* I'm using the term "ministry opportunity" broadly here. For some people, this could mean an opportunity to preach or lead worship, but for most people it will probably mean something more like an opportunity to talk to someone who looked lonely or give some money to help someone with a legitimate need. So if you jumped in and took an opportunity like that, how would you need the Spirit to empower you? Would He need to give you words to speak, boldness to say something in the first place, supernatural love and compassion?

*Question 12.* Avoid discussing what steps you could take in a hypothetical way. Take time to nail down some practical steps that you're going to begin (or have already begun) taking in order to live in the power of the Spirit.

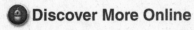**Discover More Online**

WWW.FORGOTTENGOD.COM

Missing Something?
In FORGOTTEN GOD,
breakthrough author Francis Chan returns us to the
Holy Spirit as the Bible describes Him and invites us to understand,
embrace, and follow the Holy Spirit's direction in our lives.
FORGOTTENGOD.COM
REMEMBERING THE FORGOTTEN GOD
FORGOTTEN GOD
FORGOTTEN GOD
RESOURCE YOUR SMALL GROUP WITH
Forgotten God Book
Forgotten God DVD
Remembering the Forgotten God Workbook
David C Cook
transforming lives together